T0195895

BECAUSE FEAR
WHISPERED

A book based on life stories of how we think and act apart from God's
will when fear is in control of our lives, unbeknown to us.

VANESSA WILLIAMS

authorHOUSE

AuthorHouse™
1663 Liberty Drive
Bloomington, IN 47403
www.authorhouse.com
Phone: 1 (800) 839-8640

Published by AuthorHouse 01/03/2020

ISBN: 978-1-7283-4104-0 (sc)
ISBN: 978-1-7283-4103-3 (hc)
ISBN: 978-1-7283-4102-6 (e)

Library of Congress Control Number: 2019921217

Print information available on the last page.

Any people depicted in stock imagery provided by Getty Images are models,
and such images are being used for illustrative purposes only.
Certain stock imagery © Getty Images.

Scripture taken from The Holy Bible, King James Version. Public Domain

This book is printed on acid-free paper.

Because of the dynamic nature of the Internet, any web addresses or links contained in
this book may have changed since publication and may no longer be valid. The views
expressed in this work are solely those of the author and do not necessarily reflect the
views of the publisher, and the publisher hereby disclaims any responsibility for them.

This book is written for my Boaz. Thank you for my Faith from within. I am forever grateful.

Author's Note

I feel the need to explain the way the pages are set up. They are in this order because this is the way unrecognized fear spins confusing pictures that end up as corruptive deeds in our lives and the lives of others.

It starts with what we might think is a thought of our own or a comment that we may make to ourselves. Or it might even be gossip (also not of God) said to or overheard by someone else.

The pages are set up this way to show that fear would have us believe this came from us, *but it didn't.* To prove my statement, I have provided *The Wisdom Keys* of Dr. Mike Murdock. To lay the foundation, I have grounded the pages with the words of Jesus. Jesus's prayer is the blueprint to show how the situation should have been handled from the start, with the first whisper, with godly thinking, and without heeding the poisonous whispers of fear.

Page Setup

- Fear's whisper, statement, or gossip
- The course taken with fear in control
- Explanation of the Bible verses that pertain to the situation
- The consequences
- Wisdom seeds
- Verses from Jesus's prayer (our blueprint for daily life)

INTRODUCTION

J esus's crucifixion changed life for all believers and nonbelievers alike. In most cases, each of us has gone to the cross for strength at some point in our lives. Overlooked frequently is the prayer Jesus said in the garden just before He was taken away to be crucified (John 17:1–26). Through this prayer, we should recognize that once Jesus died on the cross, we all became like Him—not only saved through his blood, but actually like Him. We have the same inheritance as Jesus! Most people go straight to the cross without stopping to look at the blueprints with the answers (the prayer). There is nothing wrong with going straight to the cross, but Jesus's prayer is an explanation of the lessons for us to gain and directions for our lives by through His death. It is a blueprint for our everyday thinking process in our lives. In most of the Bibles in my house, Jesus's prayer is divided into three sections. (The exception is a very old Bible that belonged to my grandmother.) The three sections are listed as follows.

- Jesus Prays for Himself
- Jesus Prays for His Disciples
- Jesus Prays for Future Believers

The purpose of this book is to shed some light on Jesus's prayer and show how it can be used in our everyday lives. I will show how fear is the unknown partner in not putting God first in the handling of daily dilemmas.

John 17:1–5 is labeled in the King James Version as "Jesus Prays for Himself." Recognizing that Jesus died for all, this now ends the separation from His praying for the disciples and His praying for future believers. The second part, John 17:6–19, is labeled as "Jesus Prays for His Disciples." Recognizing that Jesus wants all to go out and spread to Good News (1 Timothy 4:11–16) after His death, this makes all of us who want to be disciples for God. In John 17:20–26, the last section, "Jesus Prays for Future Believers," Jesus includes us in His plan even though we were not even born yet.

That brings me to a question: Why do we listen to fear's whispers so often?

There are two things that are failing to be recognized. One is the fact that Jesus's prayer is the blueprints for our lives. The other is that fear is whispering in our ears and controlling our daily actions. The simple fact is if one action was switched with the other, our lives would be so much better, and we could make it better for others.

For example, a man robs a bank (not living by Jesus's blueprints). He gets caught. When he is asked why he did it, he says he did it because "I wanted to!" He does not understand that fear whispered in his ear and told him that he was afraid of being poor. That one little whisper hatched the idea of robbing the bank, which led to big problems. You see, the man listened to fear instead of listening to Jesus.

This book is to unmask fear for what it is: a dastardly, deceitful, dauntless, decrepit illusionist put here by the devil to destroy the peace that Jesus died for us to have in our lives.

John 17:1–26 KJV
Jesus Prays for Himself

(1) "Father the time has come. Glorify your Son, that your Son may glorify you, (2) For you granted him authority over all people that he might give eternal life to all those you have given him. (3) Now this is eternal life: that they may know you, the only true God, and Jesus Christ, who you have sent. (4) I have brought you glory on earth by completing the work you gave me to do. (5) And now, Father, glorify me in your presence with the glory I had with you before the world began.

Jesus Prays for His Disciples

(6) "I have revealed you to those whom you gave me out of the world. They were yours; you gave them to me and they have obeyed your word, (7) Now they know that everything

you have given me come from you. (8) For I gave them the words you gave me and they accepted them. They knew with certainty that I came from you, and they believed that you sent me. (9) I pray for them I'm not praying for the world, but for those you have given me, for they are yours. (10) All I have is yours and all you have is mine. And glory has come to me through them. (11) I will remain in the world no longer, but they are still in the world, and I am coming to you Holy Father, Protect them by the power of your name-the name you gave me-so that they are not of the world. (12) While I was with them, I protected them, and kept them safe by the name you gave me. None has been lost except the one doomed to destruction so that Scripture would be fulfilled.

(13) "I am coming to you now, but I say these things while I am still in the world, so that they may have the full measure of my joy within them. (14) I have given them your word and the world has hated them, for they are not of the world any more that I am of the world. (15) My prayer is not that you take them out of the world but that you protect them from

the evil one. (16) They are not of the world, even as I am not of it. (17) Sanctify them by the truth; your word is truth; your word is truth, (18) As you sent me into the world, I have sent them into the world. (19) For them I sanctify my self, that they too may be truly sanctified.

Jesus Prays for Future Believers

(20) "My prayer is not for them alone. I pray also for those who will believe in me through their messages, (21) That all of them may be one, Father, just as you are in me and I am in you. May they also be in us so that the world may believe that you have sent me. (22) I have given them glory that you gave me, that they may be one as we are one: (23) I in them and you in me. May they be brought to complete unity to let the world know that you sent me and have loved them even as you have loved me. (24) "Father, I want those you have given me to be with me where I am, and to see my glory, the glory you have given me because you loved me before the creation of the world." (25) "Righteous Father though the world does

not know you, I know you, and they know that you have sent me. (26) I have made you known to them, and will continue to make you known in order that the love you have for me may be in them and that myself may be in them."

Chapter 1

I don't see why we have to give 10 percent of our hard-earned money to God. We worked for it. I'll give whatever I want to. It's my money, anyway.

Ubony had been on his job for twenty-five years. He had a beautiful house, five nice cars, two SUVs, and a huge heated swimming pool shaped like a *U*. He never tithed or gave more than ten dollars to any offering taken up at any church. Fear told him not to tithe. He was forever complaining about the uselessness of tithing. Ubony feared that he would not be able to pay for all his expensive things if he tithed every payday. He never could make ends meet.

One day, Ubony made a terrible mistake at work and, due to an unforgiving boss, lost his job. He was too ashamed to ask his church for money because he knew he hadn't contributed much. Ubony ended up homeless and without much of anything. He did what fear told him to do and ended up without a home and in lack of everything he was trying to keep by not tithing.

If he'd done what Jesus had prayed for in John 17:1, he would not have been afraid to ask his church for money. The authority of Jesus would have been able to show its glory to Ubony. Doing what fear told him cost Ubony his glory and his peace of mind in Jesus Christ.

Wisdom Seeds

- Your seed may leave your hand, but it will never leave your life. It goes into the future, where it multiplies.

- Your seed is a monument of trust in the mind of God.

- When your seed leaves your hand, your harvest will leave the warehouse of heaven and head toward you!

Father, the time has come. Glorify your Son,
that your Son may glorify you. (John 17:1)

Chapter 2

I want to give my life to Jesus and get saved. But I will have to stop going out and partying. My friends won't even want to be bothered with me.

J uan went out partying every weekend. His friends would pick him up from his parents' house. They'd take him out to the clubs, and then they'd get him so drunk he couldn't walk. He didn't even know he was in the world most nights. His friends used to set him on his parents' lawn, ring the door bell, and drive off while laughing. He started at age twelve, and twenty-one years later, he was in the same situation but with different (much younger) friends. After losing his wife of six years and three-year-old twins in a tragic accident in which he was driving drunk, Juan didn't have a lawn on which to sit. He walked around begging for change and spending it on the cheapest alcoholic drink he could find. Most days, he was still unsure of his own existence. Fear told him he would lose his friends if he gave his life to Jesus. John 17:2 says Jesus prays that He is the way to eternal life, and He knows of your existence. Fear lost Juan his authority over his drinking and his salvation.

- Satan is the source of all the pain you will experience during your lifetime.

- Pain is discomfort created by disorder.

- Battle is your chance for recognition, both in heaven and hell.

> For you granted him authority over all people
> that he might give eternal life to all those you
> have given him. (John 17:2)

Chapter 3

People don't have souls! When I die, I'm going to be reincarnated into whatever I want to be.

Richard is sixty-five years old. He's always had a problem with believing the Bible. He hasn't been to church for so long that he can't remember when he last attended. He's a strong believer of reincarnation. He says he's had many past lives, some that he cannot even remember. Richard had seen many of his friends die. Sad to say, none of them has resurfaced, not even in another body. Not a one has dropped in to say hi. Fear of trusting the Lord has led Richard to believe he will always come back as someone or something else. In John 17:3, Christ Jesus prays for us to know that there is only one true way to eternal life: through Him. Reincarnation is not mentioned once.

Wisdom Seeds

- Never attempt to teach a nonseeker.

- You will never win a spiritual battle logically.

- One hour in the presence of God will reveal any flaw in your most carefully laid plans.

Now this is eternal life: that they may know you, the only true God, and Jesus Christ, whom you sent. (John 17:3)

Chapter 4

The funeral was very sad. People were crying. The speaker was solemn, and there wasn't a dry eye in the room. The pianist began to play and sing "Because He Lives." The Holy Spirit told her to stand up, sing, and help bring some joy into the gloomy precession. "Glorify me and show that your soul is free! Stand up! Sing with all the joy that is inside you! This is your favorite song! There is joy in death! Give joy back to these poor souls in grief!"

D esiree just sat there, watching the grief-stricken people. She could have sent a message in her refusal to be sad and gloomy. Her message would have that the death of her wonderful aunt, Samantha, was a cause to celebrate. Samantha had helped plenty of people along the way in her life. This was not the way she would want to be remembered. This was a cause for rejoicing—one of God's own had gone to rest. But instead of standing, singing, and rejoicing, there was yelling, screaming, and crying. John 17:4–5 says for us to always bring glory to the Lord. Fear kept Desiree in her seat and kept God from being glorified.

Wisdom Seeds

- Your assignment may require you to walk away from something that is comfortable.

- Your will only be remembered for two things: the problems you solve and the ones you create.

  I have brought you glory on earth by completing the work you gave me to do. And now, Father, glorify me in your presence with the glory I had with you before the world began. (John 17:4–5)

Chapter 5

*I don't have to pay child support for her.
I'm not with her mother anymore. If I did
pay, what would my wife think?*

Alfred started out as a drug dealer in his early years. He stayed in trouble with the law and was often in and out of jail. He also fathered two daughters by two mothers. The two girls were born a month apart. About that time, he turned his life around and became a pastor. He married the mother of one of his daughters. Alfred also paid his wife's way through college. He refused to pay child support for the other daughter or help her mother in any way. Alfred let fear tell him that this child was unimportant because he was not married to her mother, so the girl really didn't exist as far as his world was concerned. Fear told Alfred to be ashamed of his own flesh and blood.

In John 17:6, Jesus prayed for Alfred to understand that he is the Lord's, and nobody can take that away from him—no one but himself. His child was growing up without a father and without support from him. Fear told Alfred to refuse his child the love that the Father had showed him. His Father has shown him love by allowing a former drug dealer to stand in the pulpit and speak on the love and support of our Father in all areas of our lives. Fear has kept a man of God from fulfilling his duties as a father and a pastor.

- Whatever you can tolerate, you cannot change.

- No one has been a loser longer than Satan.

- Never speak words that make Satan think he is winning.

I have revealed you to those whom you gave me out of the world. They were yours; you gave them to me and they have obeyed your word.

(John 17:6)

Chapter 6

I really didn't love Victoria when I married her. I still don't know if I do. She is so good with my three children, and they seem to love her. I just married her so she could help me bring them up.

Eugene met a wonderful woman. He was still carrying baggage from a marriage of eight years that had just ended. He was left with three children. One, age four, hadn't started school yet. One, five years old, had just started school. The oldest one was nine and in the fourth grade. Each one of the children, in their own way, was desperately trying to deal with the issues over the divorce of their parents and the fact that their mother was about to marry another man. Eugene met Victoria, a childless woman who opened up her heart and accepted a whole, ready-made family to love and care for. Fear told Eugene he'd found a sucker who would take care of his children while he furthered his career.

In John 17:7, Jesus prays for us to realize that whatever we have is a gift from God and should be treated as such. He ended up alone, and his children barely visited. But Victoria got to enjoy the grandchild regularly and was invited to each of the children's homes. They would even fuss about with whom she was spending the summer. Listening to fear, Eugene neglected three beautiful children and a warm-hearted, God-fearing wife for his career. That is all he ended up with.

Wisdom Seeds:

- What you love is a clue to your assignment and purpose in life.

- He multiplies your seed back into your life, where you need it most.

- Hell reacts only to your future, not your past.

- God will never advance you beyond your last act of disobedience.

Now they know that everything you have given me comes from you. For I gave them the words you gave me they accepted them. They knew with certainty that I came from you and they believed that you sent me. (John 17:7–8)

Chapter 7

Church, can you please pray for my wife and me? We have separated, and she is filing for a divorce. Also, church, I want to ask your forgiveness for a second time. I've been committing adultery.

Pastor Regney has been down this road before, looking this same congregation in their eyes and begging for forgiveness. He had brought this congregation up from a small, one-room house that was their church to a big, lovely cathedral with stained-glass windows, which had the church creed engraved in them. He'd bought lots of land around the neighborhood. They now had a food closet, which used to be a regular house in the community. Fear told Pastor Regney that he needed someone other than his wife, something other than his church responsibilities; he needed more in his life than the salvation Jesus Christ offers him even though he preaches about it almost every Sunday.

In John 17:9–10, Jesus prays about those who are not of the world. They belong to Jesus, and all Jesus has belongs to the Lord. Fear kept one of Jesus's own from believing the lessons he is preaching to his own congregation.

Wisdom Seeds:

- Obedience is the only thing God has ever required of man.

- Misery is a yesterday person trying to get along with a tomorrow God.

- If time heals, God is unnecessary.

I pray for them I'm not praying for the world, but for those you have given me, for they are yours. All I have is yours and all you have is mine. And glory has come to me through them.

(John 17:9–10)

Chapter 8

How do I know God has forgiven me for my sins? I have done so much stuff in my days—prostitution, theft, lying, adultery, cheating, and even murder. I haven't taken care of my eight children. I put them off on my mother, whose only child is me. What if I am not forgiven? What if I am not a child of God?

Patricia had run the street for most of her life. She dated only older men—mostly married men. She had fallen into prostitution in her middle twenties. She lied to most of her clients and stole from them while they were sleeping. She and the father to one of her children were in an abusive relationship. In one of their many fights, Patricia had gotten hold of a gun and shot him. He told her, "You'd better kill me. If you don't, I'm coming back to get you." He got up and started toward her, she shot him again, and that was the final blow. He was dead.

Patricia served her five years in prison. There, she turned around her life. When she got out of prison, she tried to reconnect with her children, who were all grown but one. She did find a husband. Her natural family relations were dissolved. She turned her life over to Christ, but fear made her doubt her salvation.

In John 17:11, Jesus prays for us to understand that even though we don't see Him, in His name we are one with Jesus because is Jesus is one with the Lord.

Wisdom Seeds:

- People who feel great about themselves produce great results.

- What you believe is creating your present circumstances.

- Your struggle is proof you have not yet been conquered.

- Those who created yesterday's pain do not control tomorrow's God.

I will remain in the world no longer, but they are still in the world, and I am coming to you Holy Father, Protect them by the power of your name—the name you gave me—so that they are not of the world. (John 17:11)

Chapter 9

I know the Bible. I have studied the Bible for many years. There is nothing anyone can tell me about the Bible.

D arnell was the husband of a woman who was very ill. She had diabetes. She had already lost her eyesight and was being tested to see whether her leg would need to be cut off. Even though Darnell knows what the Bible says about caring for one another just as Judas knew that Jesus was the Son of God, Darnell never fed his wife the right foods and didn't really care what she ate. He would leave her at home alone for hours on end while he ran the streets and chased other "healthy" (as he stated it) women. His wife had fallen down the stairs twice already while trying to go to the kitchen to find something to eat.

But on Sunday, Darnell was the perfect deacon. Everyone adored Deacon Darnell. He was considered a pillar to the church. Fear kept Darnell from obeying the Lord's Word on caring for his wife. Fear also told Darnell he didn't have any kind of life with a very ill wife. In John 17:12, Jesus prays that fulfillment of the scriptures is invincible.

Wisdom Seeds:

- Your seed is anything God has given you to sow into someone else.

- Whatever you have in your hand is what God will use to create your future.

- You have no right to anything you have not pursued.

- You can predict a person's future by his awareness of his assignment.

While I was with them, I protected them, and kept them safe by the name you gave me. None has been lost except the one doomed to destruction so that Scripture would be fulfilled.

(John 17:12)

Chapter 10

I'm so depressed all the time. I have no friends and nothing to live for. I hate this world. I just want to die.

Denise has a mother and a stepfather who are both alcoholics. She always had a nice attitude and a friendly disposition. She smiles often. Despite her loving ways, she still doesn't fit in. She walks to class alone, and no one will let her sit with them on the bus. At home, her stepfather wants to beat her for the smallest thing she does wrong. Sometimes she doesn't have to be doing anything at all, and he still wants to hit her. Her mother usually is too drunk and passed out on the couch. If she is awake, she simply laughs and agrees with her husband. Denise has been put out before by her stepfather "Because she looks too much like her daddy." Denise's natural father was killed in a car accident when she was three years old. She feels she has nothing to be happy about.

Fear told Denise she has no father, but in all actuality, the very joy she doesn't realize she has comes from the Father, God. In John 17:13, Jesus prays for us to keep the joy of Jesus and the Father inside us no matter the circumstances.

Wisdom Seeds:

- The broken become masters at mending.

- Champions are rarely chosen from the ranks of the unscarred.

- Your significance is not in your similarity to difference from another.

- Go where you are celebrated instead of where you are tolerated.

I am coming to you now, but I say these things while I am still in the world, so that they may have the full measure of my joy within them.

(John 17:13)

Chapter 11

That Mrs. Stewart is always so pleasant. She hugs on the kids, and they just love her! All she does is listen to that old Christian music and go to church. I hate her! She is such a Goody Two-shoes!

Mrs. Keen hates Mrs. Stewart. Mrs. Stewart has a good repetition with the children in the special education class. The children do not respond well to Mrs. Keen because she constantly criticizes them. She frequently raises her voice at them when they don't understand instructions given to them the first time. Mrs. Keen never wants to help the ones who are in wheelchairs and need assistance in the restroom. She lets them know how frustrated she is if they make any mistakes and she has to clean them off or change a diaper for them. "You kids are too old for someone to have to change your diaper! You shouldn't even be wearing them! Most of you are over fifteen years of age!" Mrs. Keen doesn't recognize their disabilities.

Mrs. Stewart, on the other hand, is always patient with them and shows the children the love and warmth that most of them don't get at home. That is why they respond to her better. Fear has Mrs. Keen frustrated and keeps her from trying to figure out what Mrs. Stewart's gift is. Jesus prays in John 17:14 for us to show what Mrs. Stewart is demonstrating: that she has the Word of God in her, and her confidence in God is showing that she is not of the world.

Wisdom Seeds:

- You have no right to anything you have not pursued.

- What you love is a clue to something you contain.

- Your daily agenda should be built around your assignment.

- Satan always attacks those he fears the most.

I have given them your word and the world has hated them, for they are not of the world any more that I am of the world. (John 17:14)

Chapter 12

I have been running for Jesus for a long time, and I'm not tired yet. Through it all, I've learned to trust in Jesus. I've learned to trust in God. I've learned to depend upon His Word.

Laroce has been a devout Christian since she can remember. She had always served the Lord in her way, her actions, and her service. She lives for the Lord. Her light shines in whatever she does and wherever she goes. She reads her Bible, teaches Sunday school, ushers in the church, and sings in the choir. She visits nursing homes, prisons, and crack houses to preach the gospel of Jesus. Her family reflects on her bringing them into the ways if the Lord. She has wonderful, smart, saved children. Laroce is living the life that Jesus prayed for. Jesus wants us to live the kind of life He spoke of in John 17:15–19. Her only fear is that she can't serve the Lord enough, but this is a fear she dutifully enjoys!

Wisdom Seeds:

- When you let go of what is in your hand, God will let go of what is in His hand.

- Faith comes when you hear God talk.

- People see what you are before they hear what you are.

My prayer is not that you take them out of the world but that you protect them from the evil one. They are not of the world, even as I am not of it. Sanctify them by the truth; your word is truth; your word is truth, As you sent me into the world, I have sent them into the world. For them I sanctify my self, that they too may be truly sanctified. (John 17:15–19)

Chapter 13

He has been gay every since he was born! I' am his sister; I am no fool! He claims he changed, and now he is an evangelist for Jesus. He says he's given his heart to Jesus. He probably only did it because Jesus was a man! And how does he know that this Jesus will accept homosexuals?

Ann's brother Dennis used to play with Ann's Barbie dolls, and he played dress-up with Ann and her friends. They would all dress up in their mom's high heels, big hats, and dresses that dragged on the floor and play, "Let's go out to the club." Then as they grew older, he'd dress in drag, with high heels (now in his size), cherry red lipstick, and tight-fitting dresses. He looked better than any women around! He was the life of every party.

Now, Ann is finding his change over to Jesus very hard to swallow. She hasn't spoken to Dennis ever since he told her he'd gotten saved and given his life to Christ. He has called her lots of times and left messages for her to join him in his new life. She won't answer her phone when she sees his name on the caller ID. Jesus prays in John 17:20–21 for those who believe to show it through their message. Fear has told Ann she's lost her brother with whom she'd partied. But it won't tell her about her brother's salvation and his happiness in the Lord. Fear is keeping her from communicating with him.

Wisdom Seeds:

- Crisis always occurs on the point of promotion.

- Crisis is merely a season for creativity.

- God never consults your past to determine your future.

- Crisis always occurs at the curve of change.

> My prayer is not for them alone. I pray also for those who will believe in me through their messages, that all of them may be one, Father, just as you are in me and I am in you. May they also be in us so that the world may believe that you have sent me. (John 17:20–21)

Chapter 14

Bryan treats his wife any kind of way. He goes out and comes home when he wants to. When he is home, he beats her; it seems like she always has to wear sunglasses. Three months ago, he broke her arm. Isn't she pregnant? Last month, he stole all her money from her paycheck as soon as she cashed it!

B ryan and Annette's marriage started out wonderfully. Bryan had a good job and was on his way to moving up to management in the company. Annette was in school and working. Along came Pearl, the new management consultant. She wormed her way right into Bryan's heart. Also, Rosie was hired on as Bryan's new assistant. Bryan thought he was on to something. He started to neglect Annette. He would be with Pearl on one night and Rosie the next. He took Rosie shopping with the money he'd stolen from Annette. He'd take Pearl out with money from the petty cash account at work—money he knew he couldn't replace. He even had sex with Pearl at work during business hours! The boss found out about his little game and fired him on the spot.

Then the beatings began for Annette. He also started making her feel as if it was her fault he'd gotten fired and it was her fault he needed other women! Annette did not understand what was going on, but she loved Bryan. She has now quit school and gotten another job to pay (not *help* pay) the bills. While she was working, Bryan was still out playing around with Pearl and Rosie. Annette finally got tired and left one day. He doesn't know where she is.

In John 17:22–23, Jesus is pointing out in his prayer that He and the Father are one, as we all are one in Christ. This is especially true for husband and wife. Fear told Bryan that he needs more than one woman, and even more than two women, in his life. Fear has lost Bryan his wife and his soul, along with the souls of Pearl and Rosie.

Wisdom Seeds:

- What you are willing to walk away from determines what God will bring to you.

- Failure is not an event but an opinion.

- Failure cannot happen in your life without your permission.

- Satan cannot linger where he is firmly resisted.

I have given them glory that you gave me, that they may be one as we are one: I in them and you in me. May they be brought to complete unity to let the world know that you sent me and have loved them even as you have loved me.

(John 17:22–23)

Chapter 15

I'm dirty, I'm hungry, and I stink. If I walk into the church, those people will laugh at me, look down on me, and treat me poorly. I think I'll stay out here on the streets with the others to save myself the humiliation.

S ean loved the Lord. He had gone to church all the time as a child and into his early adulthood. After a long bout with depression and drugs plus nine years of wrong choices in life, he stood on the steps of the very church in which he was raised. Sean wanted to go in; the music sounded so good that it warmed his heart. But he decided he did not belong. He had now adjusted to the life of the homeless. Here, he fit in among the "nothing people," as he like to all of them, himself included.

Jesus prays in John 17:24 that we should all be where He is so that the inheritance we had before any of us were born be glorified through God's love for us all no matter what the circumstances.

Fear told Sean he has no inheritance, and it made him forget what he was taught as a child and young adult about God's love. Fear turned Sean into a "nothing person" as the battle goes on in his mind.

Wisdom Seeds:

- Intolerance of the present creates a future.

- Success is satisfying movement toward worthwhile goals that God has scheduled for your life.

- Failure will last only as long as you permit it.

- Failure cannot happen in your life without your permission.

Father, I want those you have given me to be with me where I am, and to see my glory, the glory you have given me because you loved me before the creation of the world. (John 17:24)

Chapter 16

My birthday is two days before Christmas. My mom wants me to give my life to Jesus on birthday as a present to Him. Ugh! What has He given me? I'm the one locked up for His birthday! I need to ask Jesus where my birthday present is. I am not doing it, not even for her. And who ever heard of giving a present away for your own birthday, anyway?

L amar was angry that he had gotten caught robbing a house right before his birthday. He was good at what he called his trade; he'd done it numerous times. Besides that, nobody had given him anything in life, so he always stole what he wanted. This was his life, and he had gotten away with it for a long time. He thought his mom had no right asking him to give his life to anyone else.

Jesus prayed in John 17:25 for us to know Him and know that God sent Him. Fear has told Lamar that no one has the right to own his life because no one has ever given him anything. Fear has talked Lamar right out of the chance for his biggest heist: his own soul from the devil. Fear has kept him for a life more precious than silver, gold, and even platinum!

Wisdom Seeds:

- Your words are the vehicles to your future.

- Your purpose is not your decision but your discovery.

- When you say what God says, you will start to feel what God feels.

- Stop looking at what you can see and start looking at what you can have.

Righteous Father though the world does not know you, I know you, and they know that you have sent me. (John 17:25)

Chapter 17

I am not going to teach my children about any god. I'm going to let them grow up and make their own decisions. That is not my job! All I have to do is feed them and clothe them. Their religion is their responsibility. I don't need God to raise my children.

Tereona is now fifty-five years old. She was twenty-seven years old when she made that statement and lived by it. Neither she nor any of her seven children has gone to church. Out of the seven, there are only four of them still alive. Her oldest died in jail of AIDS. The next oldest was killed in a drug deal gone bad—right in Tereona's own home. She was sleeping in her bedroom when her daughter's throat was cut in the kitchen. Tereona woke to find her dead on the floor in a pool of blood. The last child Tereona had was actually the first one to die. At age thirteen, he was upset that a girl in school did not feel the same way about him that he felt about her. He got some Valium from one of his friends. The friend thought he wanted them to sell. He took all twenty-eight of them, lay down to sleep, and never woke up. He ended his life at his friend's house. Tereona is at her wits' end, not knowing whether she is going or coming.

Jesus prayed in John 17:26 for us to make the love of God known, just as God made His love for Jesus known to all. Jesus prays that we all should know that we are one in the

Lord, as is He. Fear told Tereona she did not need to fulfill her job as a parent to teach her children about the love of the Lord. Her fear of a religious connection has lost her her children—the ones who died and the ones who are still alive. The daily pain she carries inside is also shared by the lives her children live because they are in the drug game too.

Wisdom Seeds:

- God will never promote you until you become overqualified for your present assignment.

- The smallest step in the right direction always creates joy.

- God never forgets anyone who makes Him feel good.

- Proof of God's presence far outweighs the proof of His absence.

I have made you known to them, and will continue to make you known in order that the love you have for me may be in them and that myself may be in them. (John 17:26)

CONCLUSION

A few small, whispered words of fear can change our lives and the lives of people around us from good to bad. The trick of fear is to make us think that we are the only ones to blame. Yes, fear wants us to believe we thought this whole mess of trouble up by ourselves. Fear is almost never recognized for its part in the most disastrous of situations. Most times, people don't even know fear was the mastermind. Even if people do know it was fear, they don't want it to be known by anyone else that they actually fear anything; neither do they want it to be known that fear actually led them into calamity.

This book was written to expose the truth (John 8:41; John 10:10).

We are all leaders in Christ Jesus (Joshua 1:6–7).

Jesus prays in John 17:1–26 for us to be saved leaders for the Lord, just as He was in His time here on Earth. Leaders for the Lord do not think apart from God (2 Corinthians 7:1). We all have the capability to change lives for the better, for the Lord (Proverbs 22:17–21).

In all situations of life, remember that we are part of Jesus, just as Jesus is part of God (Ephesians 5:1–2). Children are part of their parents (1 Corinthians 7:14; Ephesians 6:4; Luke 11:13; Isaiah 44:3).

A husband is part of his wife (1 Corinthians 7:3–5). Through Jesus's crucifixion, we are all tied together in God. The capture, brutal beating, and finally wonderful death of Jesus saved our souls and brought us all together in our Father (John 8:29). The Holy Spirit is in us as proof of God's existence in us (1 Corinthians 12:12), just as our bodies belong to God because of the gift of the Holy Spirit from Jesus (John 20:22).

The point of Jesus's death was to save our souls and secure our ties to our Father in the Holy Ghost. These ties bind our unknown partner, who causes us to fail and refuses to take the blame, out of our minds, out of our works, and best all out of our lives (Isaiah 41:10; Psalm 112:6–7).

When our understanding is alerted, then and only then can we repent (Acts 3:19), forgive (James 5:19–20), and experience the life of fullness that Jesus was crucified for so that we could live (John 15:9–17; Mark 11:22–25; Psalm 32:7–11; Psalm 46:1–3).

Live without fear!

Acknowledgments

The Bible verses were taken from the Holy Bible, King James Version, copyright by Williams Collin Sons & Co. Ltd.

The Wisdom Keys and Decision pages were taken from *Wisdom for Crisis Times: Master Keys for Success in Times of Change* by Dr. Mike Murdock, published by the Wisdom Center, Denton, Texas.

Decision

Will you accept Jesus as your personal Savior today?

The Bible says, "That if thou shalt confess with thy mouth the Lord Jesus, and shalt believe in thine heart that God hath raised Him from the dead, thou shalt be saved" (Romans 10:9). Pray this prayer from your heart today!

Dear Jesus, I believe that You died for me and rose again on the third day. I confess I am a sinner. I need Your love and forgiveness. Come into my heart. Forgive my sins. I receive Your eternal life. Confirm Your love by giving me peace, joy, and supernatural love for others. Amen.

Cut along the dotted line and mail the bottom portion.

If this book has helped you to decide to turn your life over to Jesus, or if it has reopened your eyes the God's love for you and made you realize that He is there for you, all you have to do is reach for Him. Please help our church to continue to do the Lord's work by giving a donation to:

First Corinth Missionary Baptist Church

2165 Donald Lee Hollowell Parkway

Atlanta, GA 30318

Send us your name and address so we can send you more literature and keep you in our prayers.

NAME	BIRTHDAY

ADDRESS

CITY	STATE	ZIP

PHONE (optional)	E-MAIL (optional)

PRAYER

Hallelujah, Hosanna! Thank You, Father! Hallelujah, Hosanna! Thank You, Father! Hallelujah, Hosanna! Thank You, Father!

Heavenly Father, I thank You that I can hallow Your names this morning. I thank You for sending Your Son, Jesus the Christ, to redeem humankind, especially me, and my harvest of souls into Your kingdom. I thank You that Jesus purchased a threefold redemption for my spirit, mind, and body.

Father, I thank You that You have forgiven me, so I forgive whoever has wronged me, and I ask You to search my spirit and remove any trace of disobedience from my life. Today, I release from my mental prison anyone who has hurt me in any way. I ask You, Father, to help them spiritually.

Father, I thank You that I have the blood brought right given to me from Your Son, Jesus, dying on the cross and raising again from the dead to ask for help in all Your names. I know that You are there to come through for me. I thank You, because I have the blood bought right to have Your favor on my life. I thank You that You hear my prayers and answer! Thank You for letting me hear Your voice—and a stranger's voice I do *not* hear. I thank You that You help me to pray Your words back to You so You may bless my life and the doings therein.

Father, I thank You for blessing this bread that represents the body of Christ. I thank You that You bless this fruit of the vine that represents the precious blood of Christ.

Father, I thank You that as I receive this communion, You bring forth my reconciliation to You. I thank You that You bring strength to me spiritually, mentally, and physically because of the New Covenant that was sealed through the suffering, death, and resurrection of Jesus the Christ, which I truly believe with my whole heart!

I thank You that Jesus carried my infirmities, and therefore You lift from me all that Jesus has carried for me by the shedding of His blood, His death, and His resurrection for my life!

By faith, I thank You, Father, and receive Your blessings, favor, and the blood that bought reconciliation, given to me by my Brother, Jesus.

Father, I give You all the glory, all the honor, and all the praise in the marvelous name of Your Son, Jesus Christ, my Savior and my Brother.

I'm an heir to the kingdom! Hallelujah! Hosanna! Thank You, Father!

Amen.

Fear is the opposite of faith.

Question yourself about the fear within.

Then get rid of it.

Rely on the I Am within you.

Do not quake and quiver, nor plot on your outer sites and circumstances.

We walk by faith and not by sight.

Walk in the knowledge of the true God, I Am.

ABOUT THE BOOK

The purpose of this book is to shed some light on Jesus's prayer and show how it can be used in our everyday lives. It will also show how fear is the unknown partner in not putting God first in the handling of daily dilemmas. John 17:1–5 is labeled in the King James Version as "Jesus Prays for Himself." Recognizing that Jesus died for all, this now ends the separation from His praying for the disciples and His praying for future believers. The second part, John 17:6–19, is labeled as "Jesus Prays for His Disciples." Recognizing that Jesus wants all to go out and spread the Good News (1 Timothy 4:11–16) after His death makes all of us who want to be disciples for God. John 17:20–26, the last section, is labeled as "Jesus Prays for Future Believers." Jesus includes us in His plan, even though we were not even born yet. That brings me to a question: Why do we listen to fear's whispers so often?

Printed in the United States
By Bookmasters